CW01213179

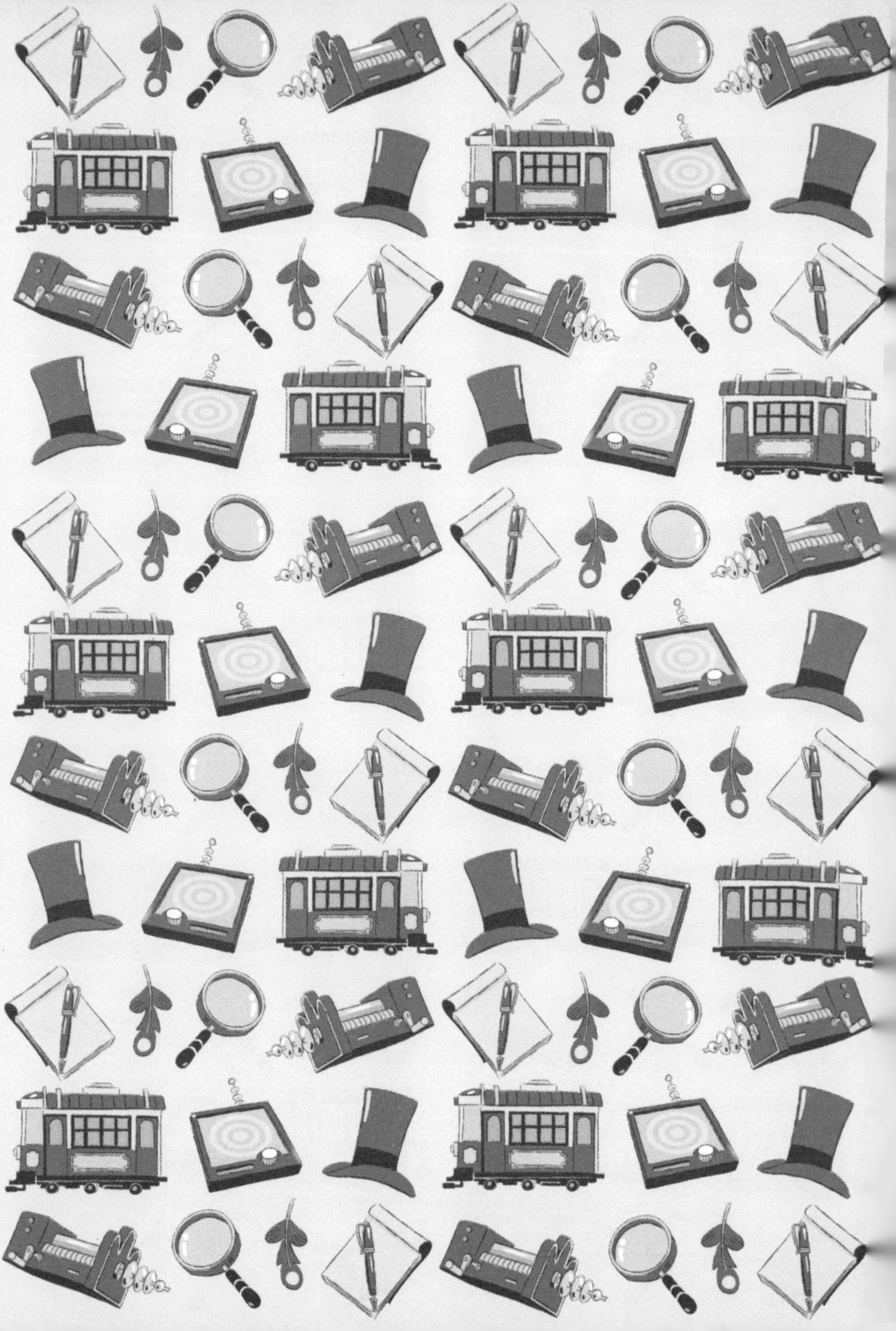

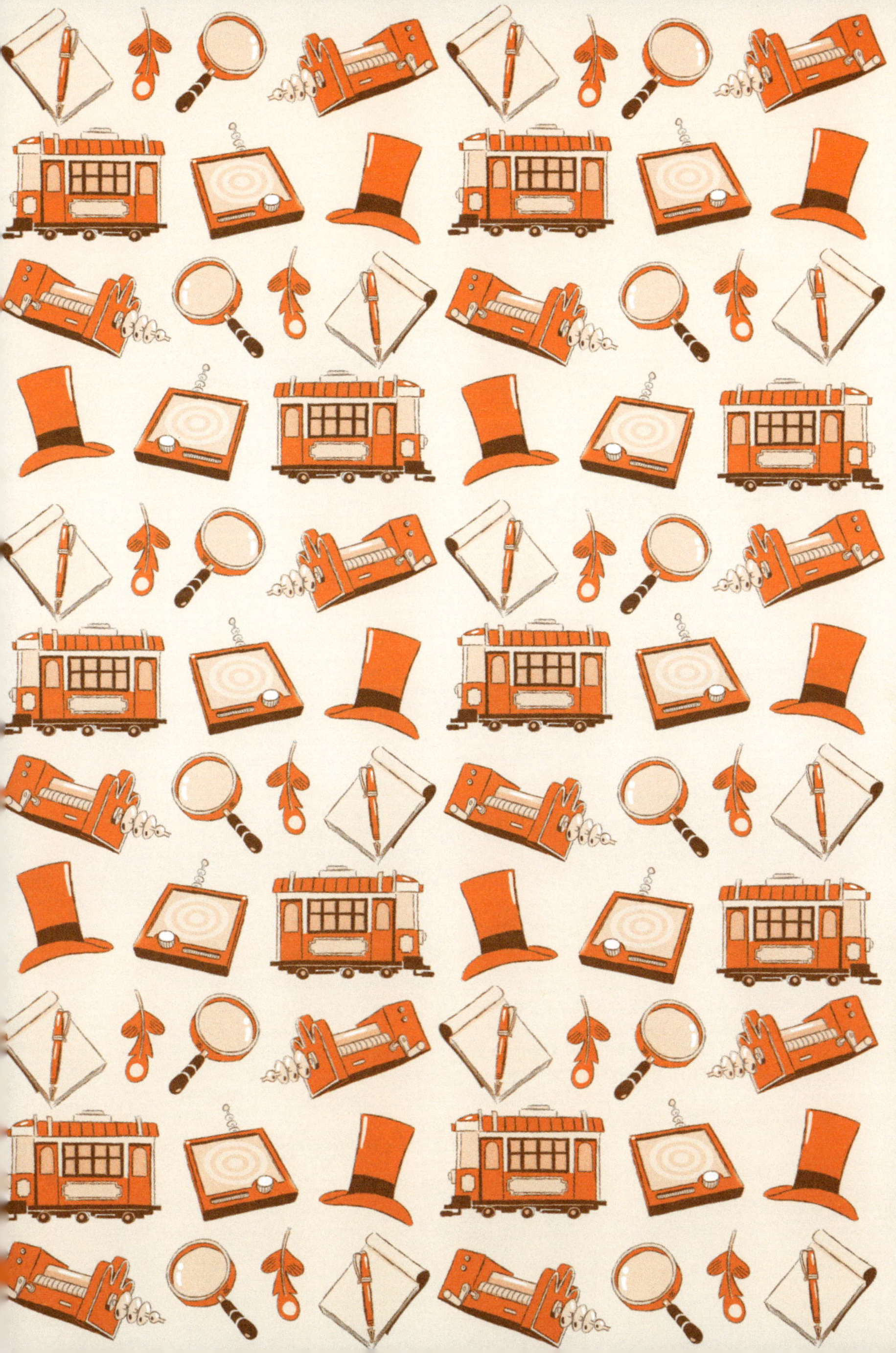

OXFORD
UNIVERSITY PRESS

Great Clarendon Street, Oxford, OX2 6DP, United Kingdom

Oxford University Press is a department of the University of Oxford. It furthers the University's objective of excellence in research, scholarship, and education by publishing worldwide. Oxford is a registered trade mark of Oxford University Press in the UK and in certain other countries

Text © Oxford University Press 2024

Illustrations © Pedro Rodriguez 2024

The moral rights of the author have been asserted

First Edition published in 2024

All rights reserved. No part of this publication may be reproduced, stored in a retrieval system, or transmitted, in any form or by any means, without the prior permission in writing of Oxford University Press, or as expressly permitted by law, by licence or under terms agreed with the appropriate reprographics rights organization. Enquiries concerning reproduction outside the scope of the above should be sent to the Rights Department, Oxford University Press, at the address above.

You must not circulate this work in any other form and you must impose this same condition on any acquirer

British Library Cataloguing in Publication Data

Data available

ISBN: 978-1-382-04374-8

10 9 8 7 6 5 4 3 2 1

The manufacturing process conforms to the environmental regulations of the country of origin.

Printed in China by Golden Cup.

Acknowledgements

Family Business and *The Case of the Curious Penguins* written by Elen Caldecott

The publisher wishes to thank Changing Faces for their valuable contribution to the development of this book. www.changingfaces.org.uk

Links to third party websites are provided by Oxford in good faith and for information only. Oxford disclaims any responsibility for the materials contained in any third party website referenced in this work.

Content on pages 9, 22, 41, 54, 66, 86, 88 and 92 written by Suzy Ditchburn

Illustrated by Pedro Rodriguez

Author photo courtesy of Elen Caldecott

Every effort has been made to contact copyright holders of material reproduced in this book. Any omissions will be rectified in subsequent printings if notice is given to the publisher.

MIX
Paper | Supporting responsible forestry
FSC www.fsc.org FSC™ C110497

Family Business

Written by Elen Caldecott
Illustrated by Pedro Rodriguez

OXFORD
UNIVERSITY PRESS

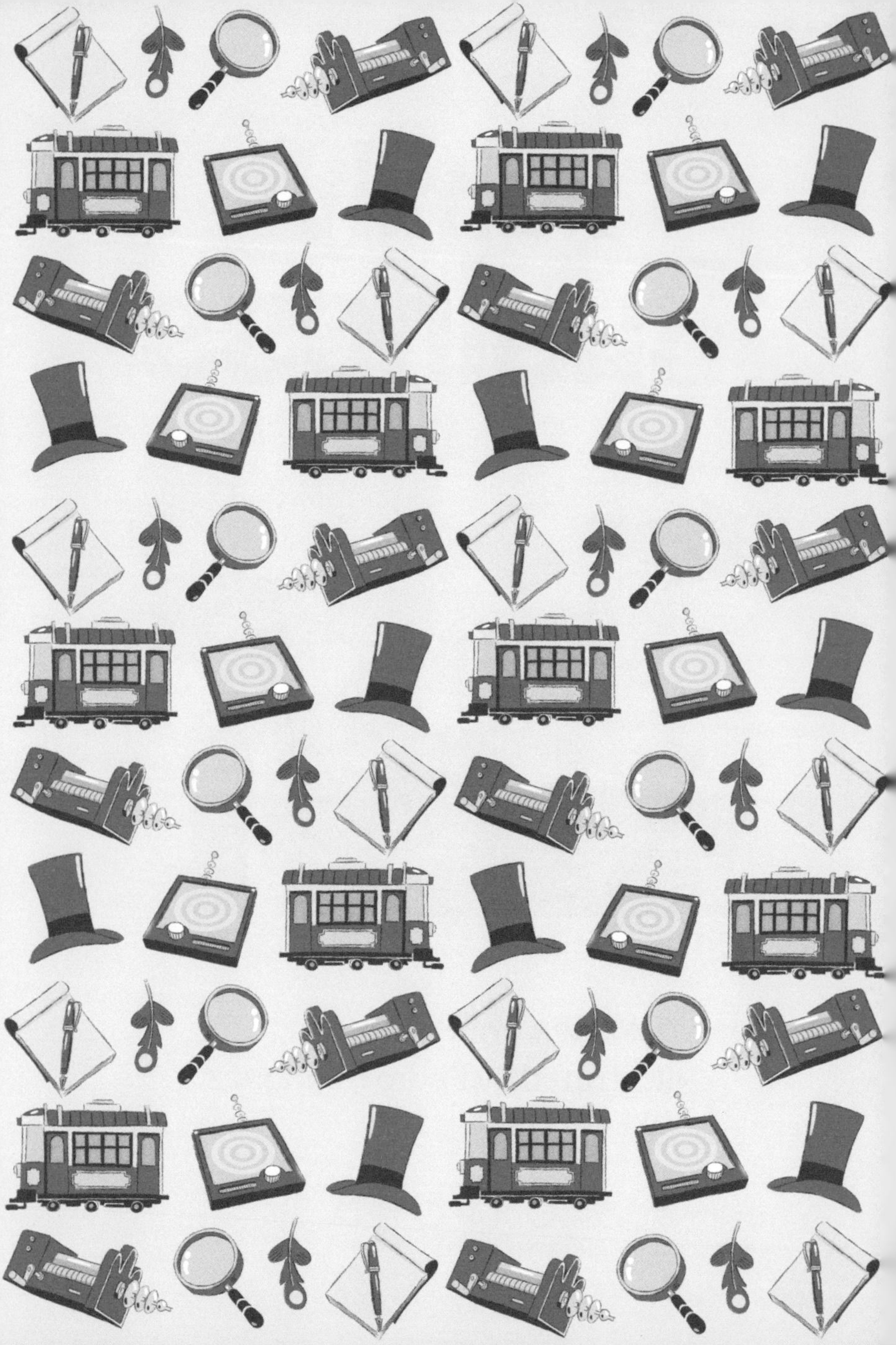

Read this book if ...

you like

SOLVING MYSTERIES

and want to be a

DETECTIVE!

8

STOP AND THINK

In this book, you'll see how the Hoodunnit family of detectives try to solve the crime of the missing Ice Blaster.

What do you know about a detective's job? What skills do you think you need to be a good detective?

The Hoodunnit Detective Agency

Solving crime is the family business!

Ms Azelina Hoodunnit – Founder (Mum)

Calum and Maddie Hoodunnit (the twins) – Senior Detectives

Francis Hoodunnit – Very Junior Detective

Chapter 1
Cold case

Francis Hoodunnit crouched outside his mother's office door. He was listening secretly.

'Francis!'

Mum called sharply.

'I can see the tip of your toe. If you are going to eavesdrop, do it properly.'

Francis **whipped** his foot back, feeling cross with himself.

He took out his notebook and jotted down a note.

Remember feet when hiding.

Just then, Mum's phone **rang**.

'Hoodunnit Detective Agency, how can I help?' Mum said. 'Oh dear. Straight away. Goodbye!' She put down the phone.

'Hoodunnits!'

she shouted. 'We've got a case!'

Footsteps
    clattered
        on the
            stairs.

The twins **hurtled** past Francis.

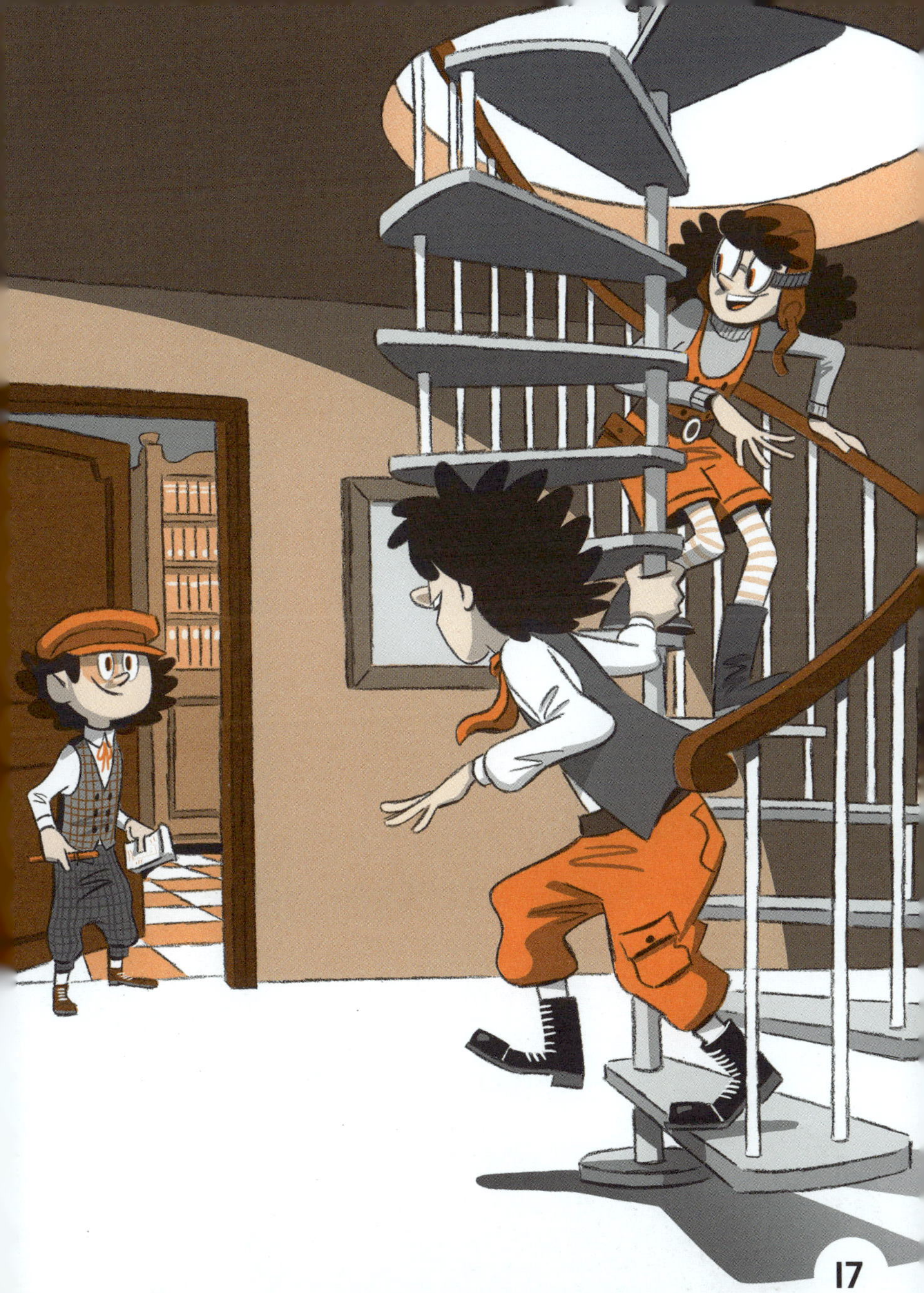

'The Ice Blaster has disappeared from the museum,' Mum said. 'It's a powerful **FREEZING** device. It is used to stop ice melting. In the wrong hands, it could cause **chaos**.'

'Powerful?' thought Francis. 'Chaos?' He **wriggled** with excitement.

'I need you two to investigate,' Mum told the twins.

'Do you mean "**you three**"?' Francis asked, hopefully.

Calum pulled a face. '**Muuum**,' he moaned. 'We can't investigate <u>and</u> babysit.'

'I don't need babysitting!' Francis said crossly.

'I can help. I'm a **Hoodunnit**, too!'

Mum nodded thoughtfully.

'It's time you had a chance,' she said.

'Twins, take your little brother with you.

Francis, it's crucial you **listen** to Calum and Maddie.'

'Just stay quiet,'

Maddie warned.

Francis mimed zipping his lips.

He was going to be a detective!

Look back

1. Why do you think the twins didn't want their little brother, Francis, to come, too?

2. Why was Francis excited about the news of the missing Ice Blaster?

3. Do you think Francis will be a good detective? Why or why not?

4. Which word in Chapter 1 means 'ran fast'?

Chapter 2
Museum mystery

They caught a tram to the museum. Francis tried to sit quietly, but it was **hard**.

'Who took the Ice Blaster?' Francis asked Maddie.

'Where do you think it is now?' he asked Calum.

The twins **ignored** him.

The museum director greeted them when they arrived.

'I'm Dr Newfangled,' she said.

'**We're** the Hoodunnit detectives,' announced Francis. Maddie glared at him.

'Come this way,' Dr Newfangled replied **sternly**.

Dr Newfangled **rushed** them through the museum. They passed displays on light and sound, on electricity and space travel.

They *hurried* past dinosaurs and mammals and birds.

'What can you tell us?' Maddie asked excitedly.

'The Ice Blaster **RE-FREEZES** melting glaciers,' Dr Newfangled explained. 'It's part of our display on **climate-care machines**. These machines are used to change the weather. Our cleaning staff discovered the **theft** this morning.'

At the gallery door, Francis gawped. He spotted a **Rain-o-matic**, a **Tempest-Tamer** and a **Sunshine-Spreader**.

Sunshine-Spreader

Ice Blaster

31

The Ice Blaster was gone!

Maddie and Calum moved straight to the empty space. Maddie took out a magnifying glass. Calum dusted for fingerprints.

'What should I do?' Francis asked.

'Stay quiet,' Maddie replied.

It wasn't fair!

He was there to investigate, too.

Francis searched. He **sniffed**.
'What's that smell?' he asked.

Was it fish?

The twins ignored him.
'There are **NO fingerprints**,' Calum said. 'The thief must've worn gloves.'
Francis was about to speak, when Maddie **yelped**.

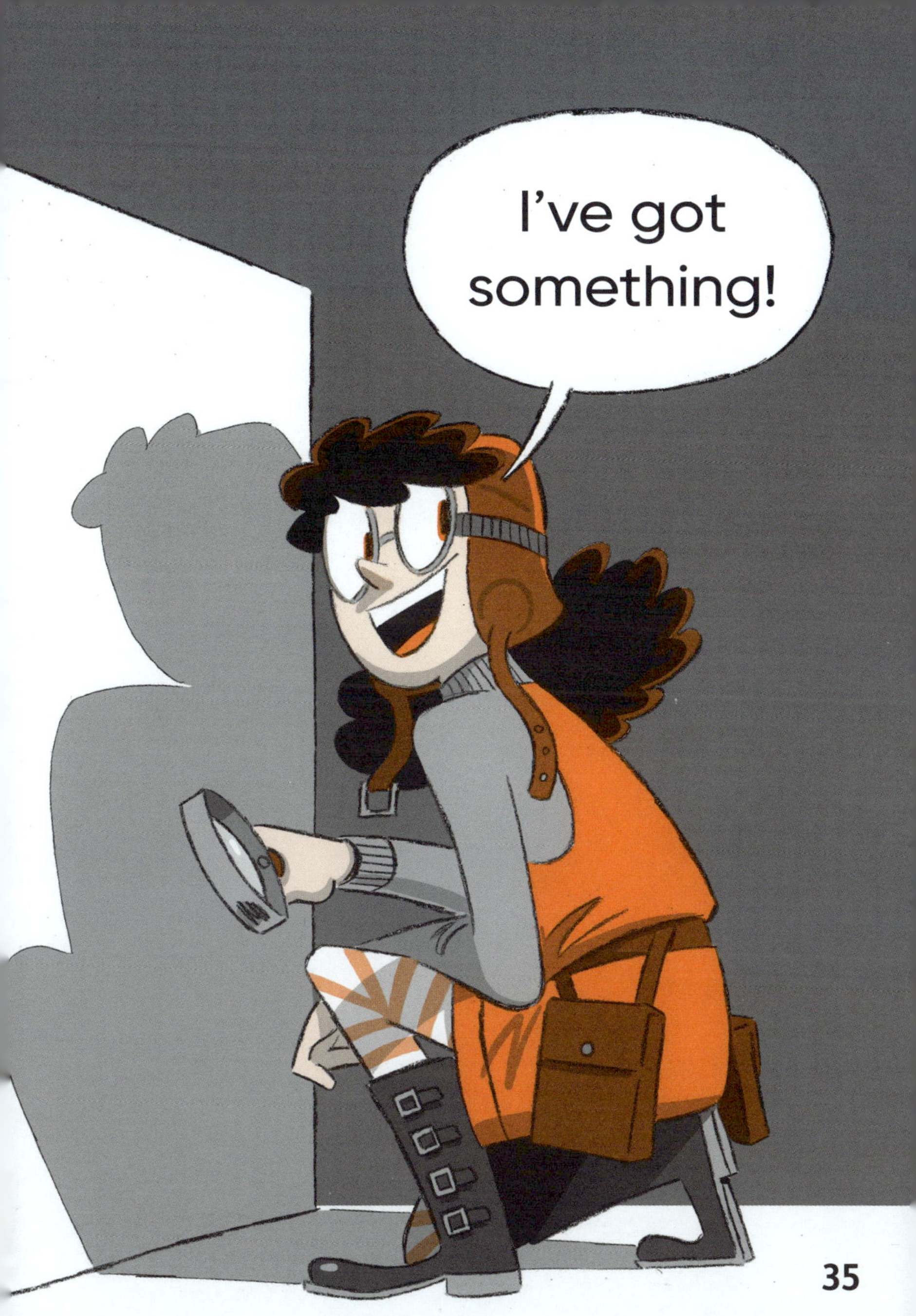
I've got something!

Maddie lifted up a small **feather**.

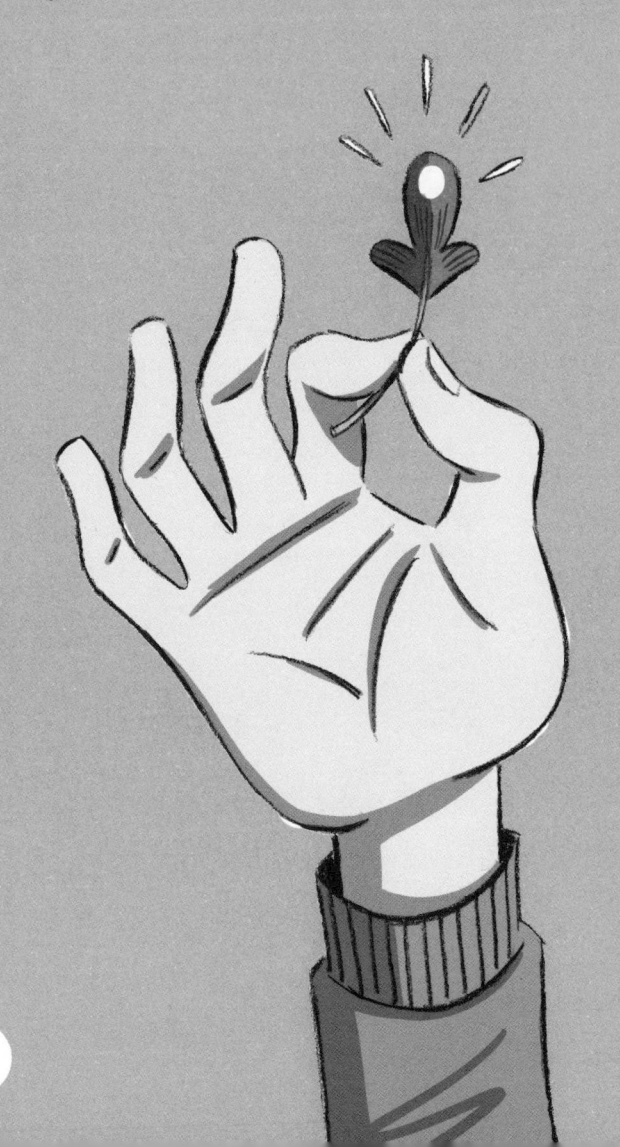

Dr Newfangled **peer**ed at the **feather**. 'That's from an *Olympus bird*,' she said.

'Where did it come from?' Maddie asked.

'We **<u>don't</u>** have any Olympus birds in the museum,' Dr Newfangled said, frowning. 'They **<u>don't</u>** live in this country. They're *tropical* birds.'

'Why would a *tropical* bird want the Ice Blaster?'

Calum wondered.

'How could a bird even steal it?'

Maddie added.

'Olympus bird **feathers** are sometimes used to **decorate** hats,' Dr Newfangled said. 'Perhaps the thief wore a fancy hat.'

'We should interview a **hatmaker**,' Maddie said.

Francis wondered again about the smell. 'What about the **fishiness?**' he insisted.

'It's probably someone's lunch,' Maddie said.

Francis wasn't sure, but he was only a **junior detective**. So, he thanked Dr Newfangled, then followed the twins out of the museum.

Next stop: the **hatmaker**.

Look back

1. Why did the twins get irritated with Francis?

2. Do you think the fishy smell Francis noticed is important? Why or why not?

3. What do you think of their feathery hat idea?

4. Find a word in Chapter 2 that means 'looked closely'.

Chapter 3
The hatmaker

Everyone knew that the **best** hatmaker in town was Mr Topper. His shop was in the *fashion* area. So, the Hoodunnits got on the tram. As they travelled closer, Calum and Maddie discussed the plan.

'Mr Topper will know whether the **feather** came from a hat,' Calum said.

'He might even know whose hat it came from,' Maddie added.

'**Why** would anyone want the Ice Blaster?' Francis wondered aloud.

'**What** would they do with it?'

The twins **ignored** him.

The tram stopped outside Mr Topper's shop. As they went inside, the sounds of the street faded. Instead, Francis heard music playing from an **old radio**. He **gazed** about.

The shop was **jam-packed** with hats. There were berets and bonnets, flat caps and fezzes.

'How can I help?'
asked Mr Topper.

'Do you recognize <u>this</u>, please?' Maddie asked. She handed over the **feather**.

'Ah. An **Olympus bird feather**.' Mr Topper said. 'I haven't seen one this fresh for years.'

'Fresh?' Calum asked.

Mr Topper examined the **feather** closely. 'Yes, I'm sure. This was gathered from a live bird recently – perhaps only yesterday. Someone must have brought it from a tropical country. How odd! It would be a **very difficult** task.'

The radio **CRACKLED**.

> That was music from the Jawbones Jazz Orchestra. Now, the weather.

'So, you **don't** think the **feather** came from a hat?' Calum asked. It was clear that he was **disappointed**. Francis understood – the **feather** was their **only** clue.

'I don't,' Mr Topper replied.

... We must inform listeners that snow has blown in suddenly ...

Francis was alert straight away.
'Sudden snow?' he thought.

'Calum! Maddie!'
Francis exclaimed.

'Not now, Francis,'
Calum said.

'Francis,' Maddie scolded, 'Mum told you to **listen** to us.'

'Listen to the radio!'
Francis shouted.

Look back

1. Why did Francis want Maddie and Calum to listen to the radio?

2. Who do you think is the best detective so far and why?

3. Why can't the feather have come from a hat?

4. Find a word in Chapter 3 that means 'full'.

Chapter 4
On thin ice

... **Reports of heavy snow are causing concern ...**

'The person who stole the Ice Blaster has switched it on,' Francis deduced. 'They are **FREEZING** the town!'

Maddie pulled out her mapping screen. 'I can search for the **COLDEST** area,' she said. 'That's where the Ice Blaster must be.'

With a few clicks, Maddie had a map showing the temperature of the town. Where the town was **COLDER**, the map was **darker**. Right at the **darkest** spot was the animal sanctuary.

Francis **gasped**. Someone at the sanctuary had the Ice Blaster! Could that person have accidentally carried the feather to the museum?

'Is there an **Olympus bird** at the animal sanctuary?' Francis asked.

'**Yes!**' Mr Topper exclaimed.

Francis' brain whirred. Maybe the thief looked after the Olympus bird. Now **why** would they want **COLDER** weather? Olympus birds lived in *tropical* climates.

Unless the keeper looked after other birds ...

Francis remembered the smell. Which birds liked **fish** – and **ICE** ...?

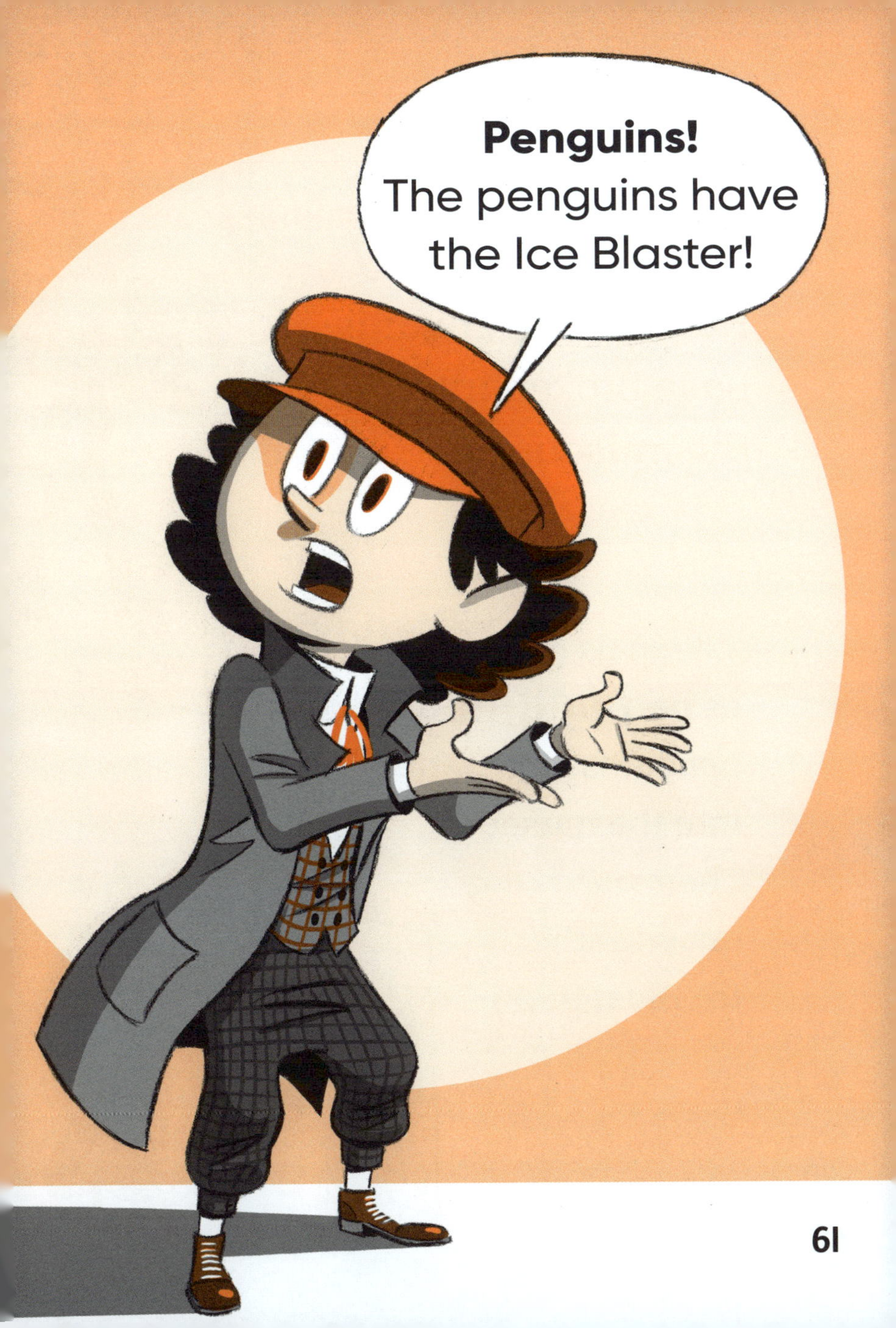
Penguins!
The penguins have the Ice Blaster!

Maddie tutted.

'Don't be silly. How could penguins have broken into the museum?'

Francis grinned as he **imagined** penguins *sneaking* into the museum. Then *sneaking* out with the Ice Blaster.

63

'**Francis!**' Maddie interrupted his daydream.

'Sorry,' Francis snapped to attention. 'No, I **don't** think the penguins are responsible for the theft. I think their **keeper** is.'

Calum and Maddie frowned. Francis could tell that they weren't sure.

'Remember the fishy smell?' said Francis. 'Perhaps the keeper wore their work gloves so they didn't leave **fingerprints**. They would smell of fish from feeding the penguins.'

Calum **nodded**. 'Let's see if you're right. Time to visit the animal sanctuary!'

Look back

1. Why are Calum and Maddie starting to listen to Francis?

2. Do you think that Francis' theory about the penguin keeper is correct? Explain why or why not.

3. Explain what the phrase 'snapped to attention' means.

Chapter 5
The sanctuary worker

On the tram to the animal sanctuary, the air tasted of **FROST**. Calum handed Francis a scarf. 'We can't have the youngest detective getting cold,' he said.

Maddie **huffed**. 'He's <u>not</u> a detective yet.'

It grew **COLDER** the closer they got to the animal sanctuary.

The ticket booth was empty.
A sign said, 'Closed due to snow!'.

The detectives *rushed past*.

They were searching for the penguins.

Francis spotted a **cheetah**.
It was doing laps of its enclosure to keep warm.

A troop of monkeys **huddled together**.

There, at the picnic tables in the middle of the animal sanctuary, were the penguins!

They slid on their bellies with **glee**.

They leaped in **delight**.

They frolicked with **joy**.

A man in a boiler suit stood on one of the tables. Francis could just make out his name badge – 'Dave Onion, keeper'. Dave was using the Ice Blaster! He fired snow over the penguins.

'HEY! STOP THERE!'

Maddie yelled.

Dave froze. Then he jumped off the table and started to *run*.

However, the ground was **too slippery**.

He **slipped** ...

he **spun** ...

he **flopped**.

His legs **flew out** from under him.

He pinged around like a pinball.

Finally, he came to a stop in front of Maddie. The Ice Blaster fell from his hands.

'Ooowwww!

That hurt,'

Dave Onion moaned.

Maddie picked up the Ice Blaster. She passed it to Calum, who put it safely inside his backpack.

The penguins **squawked** sadly as the snow stopped.

'Why did you take the Ice Blaster?' Maddie demanded.

'It was for the penguins' benefit!' Dave whimpered. 'They wanted to explore, but they couldn't unless it was **COLD** enough.'

'How did you steal it?' Calum asked.

'I strolled into the museum with the cleaners.' Dave said. 'It worked **perfectly**!'

'But you've affected the other animals.' Calum pointed at the **shivering** giraffes. 'Look! They're **miserable**.'

He pointed at the **trembling** Olympus bird.

Dave Onion looked **sheepish**. 'I'm sorry,' he said. 'I didn't mean to upset the animals!'

'Go and get blankets to keep them warm,' Maddie told him sternly. 'Your boss is on their way.'

Dave Onion did as he was told.

Maddie and Calum looked at Francis.

'**You were right**,' Maddie said. 'The keeper <u>**was**</u> responsible for the theft.' She smiled proudly. 'It seems you might be a **good detective** after all.'

'Well, he *is* a **Hoodunnit**,' Calum said.

Francis was too **pleased** to say anything at all.

Look back

1. How did the animals cope with the cold weather at the animal sanctuary?

2. What was wrong with Dave's plan to help the penguins?

3. How did they warm the animals up?

4. How did Maddie's opinion of Francis change throughout the story?

Ha! Ha!

Why did the penguins like the Ice Blaster?

Because it was brrrr-illiant!

Read out loud

This is a poem about the penguins in the story.

Read the poem to yourself and think about how you should say it and where it rhymes. Practise saying it to yourself to get into the rhythm of it.

The Case of the Curious Penguins

poem

When the curious penguins wanted to explore,

They couldn't just simply walk out of the door.

The air was too sticky, the sun was too hot!

So, the keeper, Dave, he hatched a cool plot.

He'd use an Ice Blaster to chill the air down,

Giving the penguins the run of the town.

But Dave and the penguins forgot about Francis,

The junior detective who sought all the answers.

Daring and clever, determined and bold,

Francis and the twins saved the town from the cold.

Read it again

1. After performing the poem, think about whether you can do anything differently. Perhaps you could add actions to support the meaning.

2. Try memorizing the poem so that you can say it without needing the book.

93

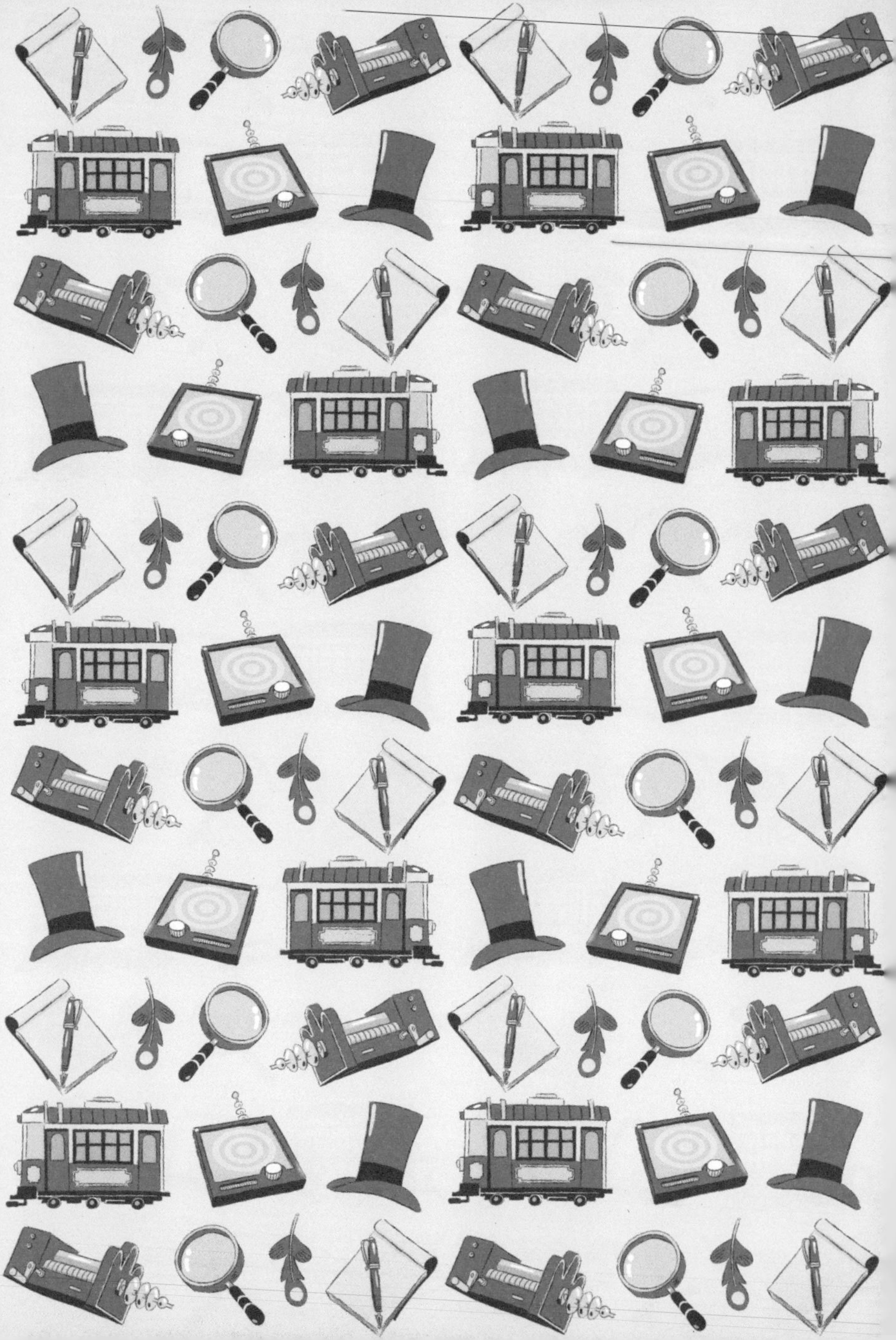

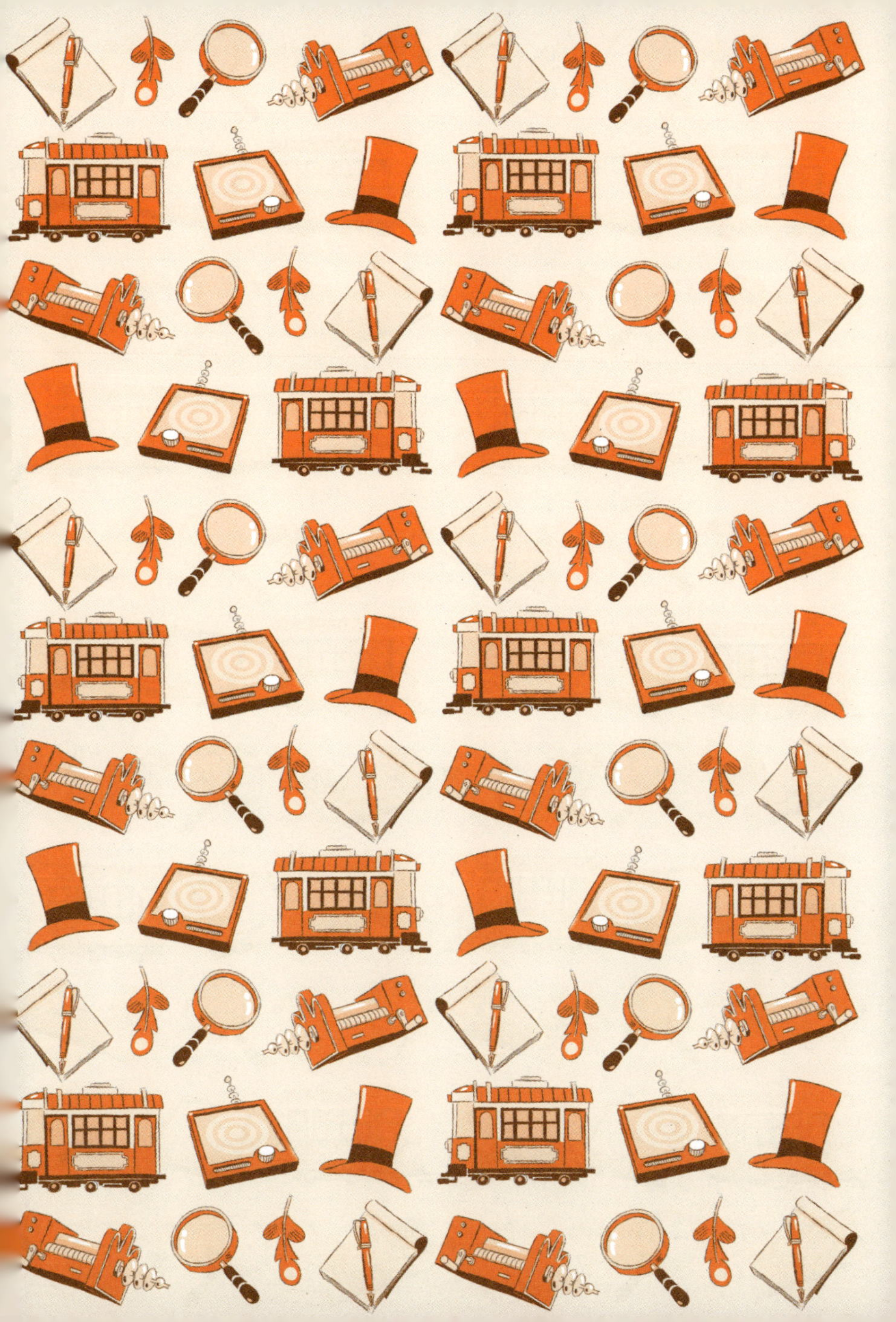

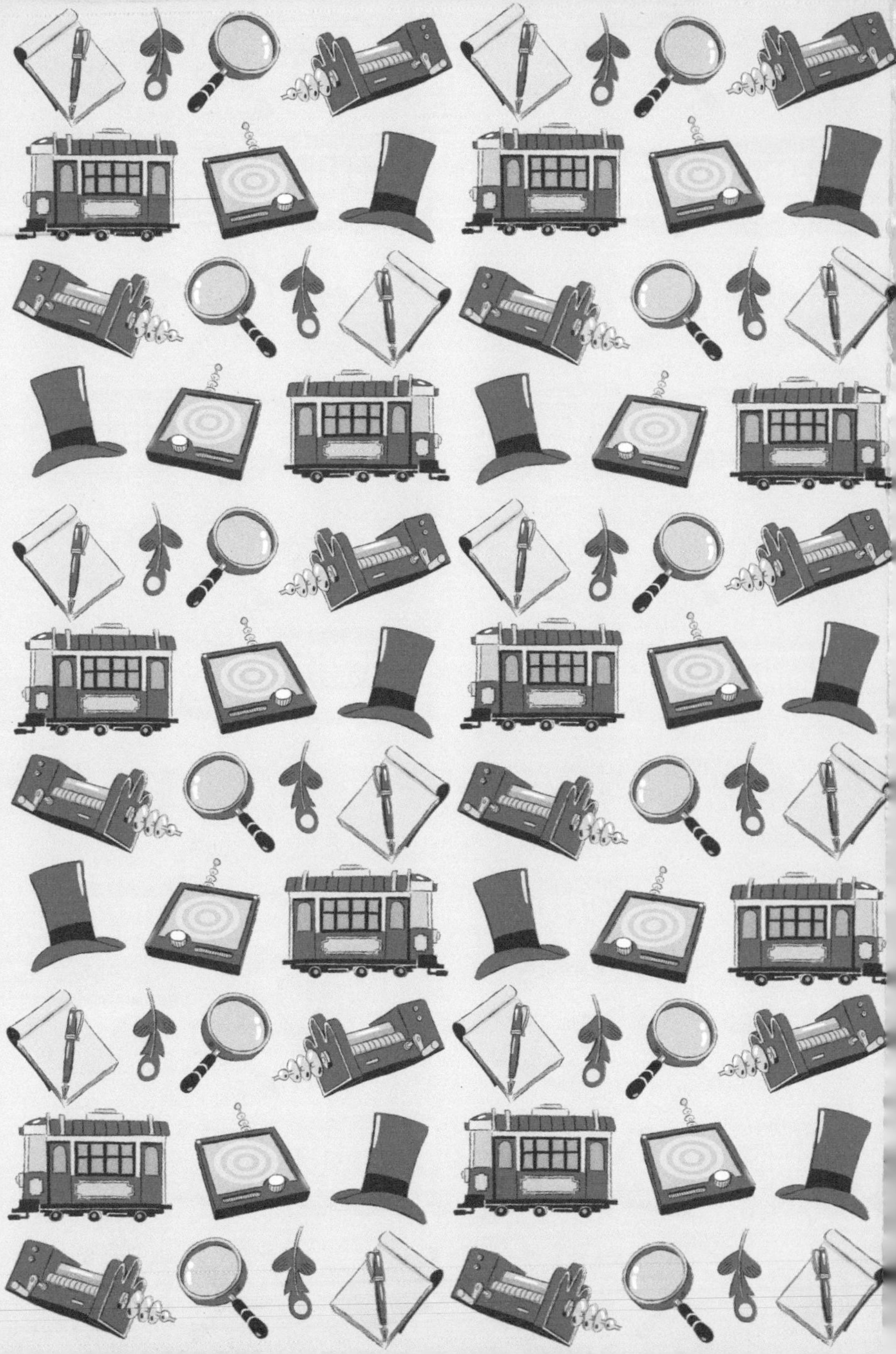